ELEPHANTS

A TRUE BOOK

by
Melissa Stewart

A Division of Scholastic Inc.

New York Toronto London Auckland Sydney
Mexico City New Delhi Hong Kong
Danbury, Connecticut

An elephant
reaching for food

Reading Consultant
Nanci R. Vargus, Ed.D.
*Teacher in Residence
University of Indianapolis
Indianapolis, Indiana*

Content Consultant
Kathy Carlstead, Ph.D.
Honolulu Zoo

*Dedication:
To Colin Campbell Stewart*

*The photograph on the cover
shows an elephant cow and
calf. The photograph on the
title page shows a herd of
African elephants.*

Library of Congress Cataloging-in-Publication Data

Stewart, Melissa
    Elephants / by Melissa Stewart.
       p. cm. — (A true book)
    Includes bibliographical references and index.
    Summary: Briefly describes the physical characteristics, habits, and behavior
of elephants, as well as some threats to their existence.
    ISBN 0-516-22199-X (lib. bdg.)   0-516-26990-9 (pbk.)
    1. Elephants—Juvenile literature. [1. Elephants. 2. Endangered species.]
I. Title. II Series.
QL737.P98 S744 2002
599.67—dc21   2001047431

SCHOLASTIC and associated designs are trademarks and/or registered trademarks of Scholastic Inc. CHILDREN'S PRESS, TRUE BOOKS, and A TRUE BOOK
and all associated designs are trademarks and/or registered trademarks of
Grolier Publishing Company, Inc.
1 2 3 4 5 6 7 8 9 10 R 11 10 09 08 07 06 05 04 03 02

Contents

An African grasslands
elephant

The Largest Land Animal

An elephant is a huge animal with gray skin, a long trunk, and big, floppy ears. The largest elephants are more than 11 feet (3.4 meters) tall and weigh about 12,000 pounds (5,443 kilograms). These elephants live on grasslands in central and East Africa. Their rounded ears

5

are as large as a blanket. Their tusks weigh about as much as you do. Some African elephants live in forests. They are a bit smaller and have longer, straighter tusks.

Asian elephants look quite a bit different from their African

An Asian elephant

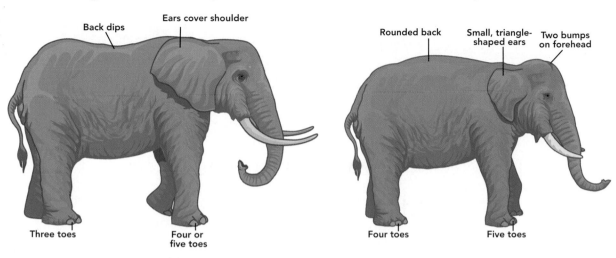

African grasslands elephant

Back dips

Ears cover shoulder

Three toes

Four or five toes

Asian elephant

Rounded back

Small, triangle-shaped ears

Two bumps on forehead

Four toes

Five toes

cousins. They are usually no more than 9 1/2 feet (2.8 m) tall and weigh about 8,000 pounds (3,629 kg). They have lighter skin, two bumps on their fore-head, and a rounded back. Their ears are small and triangle-

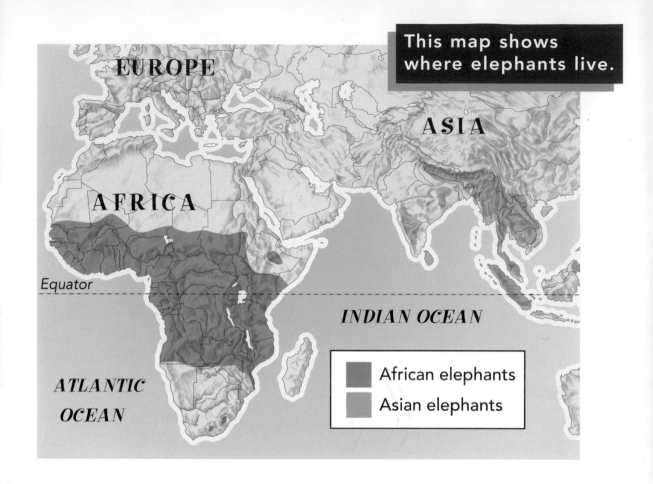

EUROPE

ASIA

AFRICA

Equator

INDIAN OCEAN

ATLANTIC
OCEAN

This map shows
where elephants live.

African elephants

Asian elephants

shaped. No female Asian elephants and only some males
have tusks. Asian elephants live
in the tropical rain forests of
India and Southeast Asia.

Elephants are the largest animals that live on land. Most animals, including humans, stop growing when they become adults. Elephants keep on growing as long as they live. The largest elephants are the oldest elephants.

Which of these elephants do you think is the oldest?

A calm elephant holds its ears flat against its body (left). An angry or frightened elephant holds its ears out straight (right).

It's easy to tell how an elephant feels. When an elephant feels calm and safe, it holds its ears flat against its body. When an elephant is angry or frightened, it holds its ears out straight. When two elephants are happy to see each other, they flap their ears, click their tusks, and make rumbling noises. They also may wrap their trunks together or lift their trunks in the air and touch each other on the forehead.

These elephants are greeting each other.

Trunks and Teeth

An elephant's trunk can be longer than a man is tall. It has no bones, but contains more than 100,000 muscles. It is strong enough to lift an object that weighs more than 100 pounds (45 kg) and sensitive enough to pluck a delicate flower out of the ground.

An elephant can use its trunk to grab high branches (left), carry heavy objects (top right), or suck up water and then squirt it into its mouth (bottom right).

An elephant's trunk is a cross between a hand and a nose. It can grab branches

20 feet (6 m) above the ground, and it can smell sweet bananas or figs more than 2 miles (3 kilometers) away. An elephant also uses its trunk to breathe, trumpet warning calls, and gather food.

An elephant trumpeting a warning call

Elephants resting in the shade

An adult elephant eats about 300 pounds (136 kg) of plant material every day. Most elephants feed in the morning and late afternoon. They rest in the mid-afternoon, when the sun is at its hottest.

Every day, elephants travel in search of food.

During the rainy season, food and water are easy to find. Each day, elephants travel about 6 to 9 miles (9.6 to 14.5 km) in search of food. During the dry season, elephants must travel farther to find food and water. Some may travel up to 30 miles (48 km) each day.

An elephant does not chew its food like you do. Instead of lifting its teeth up and down, an elephant grinds its four molars back and forth.

You will have two sets of teeth during your life—baby teeth and permanent teeth. An elephant has six sets of teeth. When one set wears out, a new and larger set grows in.

An elephant's final teeth are about 12 inches (30 centimeters) long and weigh about

10 pounds (4.5 kg) each. If an elephant lives to be more than about 60 years old, its last set of molars wears out, and the animal dies of starvation.

Many elephants also have two tusks—long front teeth that keep growing throughout the animal's life. Elephants use their tusks to defend them-selves from enemies, to knock over small trees and peel off the bark, and to dig for water, roots, and salt.

An elephant's two tusks are never exactly the same size.

An elephant's two tusks are never exactly the same. One is always shorter because the animal uses it more. Just as people are right-handed or left-handed, an elephant can be right-tusked or left-tusked.

All About Elephants

The earliest relative of the elephant lived about 45 million years ago. At one time, about 350 kinds of elephants lived in Europe, Asia, Africa, and the Americas. Today, elephants exist only in Asia and Africa.

You might be surprised to learn that the closest living

The hyrax, a mammal that is only about 12 to 20 inches (30 to 50 cm) long, is the closest living relative of the elephant.

relative of the elephant is a small animal called the hyrax. An elephant and a hyrax don't look alike on the out-side, but their insides are a different story. Some of their bones and organs look almost exactly the same— except for their size.

The elephant and the hyrax both belong to a larger group of animals called mammals. Cats, mice, and humans are mammals too. All mammals have a backbone that supports their body and helps them move. They also have lungs and breathe air. They are warm-blooded animals, so their body temperature stays about the same no matter how cold or warm their surroundings are.

An elephant
calf nursing

Baby mammals grow inside
their mother until they are
ready to be born. Then they
feed on mother's milk until
they are ready for solid food.

Elephant calves begin eating plants when they are about 6 months old.

A baby elephant may nurse for more than 2 years.

All mammals have one more thing in common—hair. You might think that an elephant has no hair, but it does

Hair on the face of an Asian elephant (above) and on the tail of an African grasslands elephant (right)

have some around its ears, eyes, and mouth. An elephant also has a bunch of thick hairs at the end of its tail.

Elephant Families

An elephant family usually consists of ten to fifteen related females, or cows, and their babies, or calves. The oldest, wisest cow leads the group. She is called the matriarch.

The matriarch decides when the group will feed and when it will rest. She knows where to find trees with tasty fruit and how to locate water during droughts.

Elephant families sometimes join together to form large, temporary herds. When male elephants, or bulls, are about 10 years old, they leave their family. They may live alone or form a loose group with other bulls.

A matriarch (center) stands in front of her family as a bull (left) greets them.

An Elephant's Life

When a female elephant is about 12 years old, she can have young of her own. Some cows have as many as ten calves during their lifetime.

Male elephants become adults at about the same age as females, but only the largest, strongest bulls have a chance

An angry
musth bull

to mate with females. When
bulls are about 25 years old,
they begin to enter a state
called musth for a few months
every year. During musth, a

dark, oily liquid with a strong
smell flows out of glands on a
bull's forehead. The male
becomes stronger and tougher
than usual. He walks with his
head held high and flaps his

ears to spread the strong scent of the liquid streaming down his face. Elephants do not fight often, but a small musth bull can successfully challenge a larger bull that is not in musth.

These young male elephants are playfighting. They will need this skill when they get older.

Female elephants usually choose to mate with males that are in musth. About 22 months later, a brown, hairy calf is born. Within 15 minutes, the newborn shakily stands up and begins to drink its mother's milk. About an hour after the baby is born, the family starts to move again. They travel slowly for a few days until the calf's legs are strong enough to keep up.

An elephant calf finds a shady spot beneath its mother's body.

An elephant calf must kneel down to drink until it learns to control its trunk.

A calf begins to eat plants when it is about 6 months old. It learns what to eat and how to act by watching adult elephants. A newborn often trips over its own trunk and may suck on it for comfort. A calf must kneel down to drink until it learns to control its trunk.

Young elephants like to play. They charge one another, butt heads, wrestle, climb on top of one another, and roll in mud.

These young elephants are playing in the mud.

Sometimes adults get silly too. They chase one another, throw plants, and spray one another with water.

Elephants are very intelligent, caring, and loyal animals. Sisters and aunts help raise calves. When a predator approaches, the entire family forms a protective circle around the youngsters. If an elephant gets sick, its family brings it food. When an elephant dies, its family covers

Elephant family members work together to protect and care for calves.

the body with tree branches and some stay close by for a couple of days.

Elephants in Danger

People have been hunting elephants for thousands of years. Most of these hunters did not eat the elephants' meat or use their hides. All they wanted were the animals' ivory tusks. Jewelry and figurines made of ivory are prized for their beauty, so ivory is very valuable.

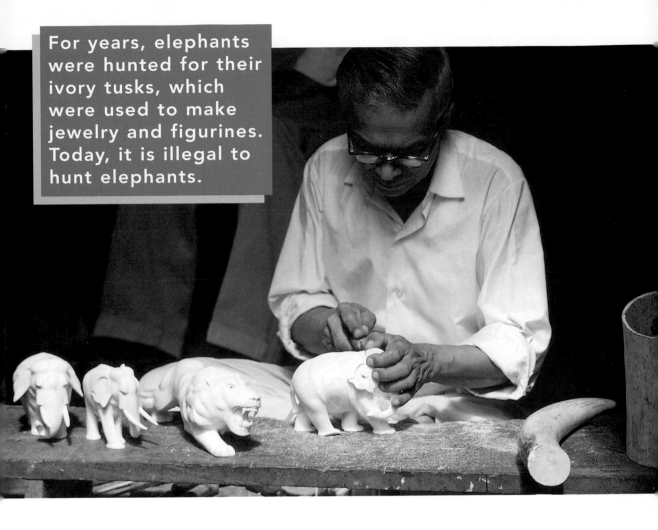

For years, elephants were hunted for their ivory tusks, which were used to make jewelry and figurines. Today, it is illegal to hunt elephants.

In the 1980s, scientists announced that if elephants were not protected from human hunters, they would all be dead by 2000. Many people were upset by this news and worked to get a worldwide ban on the sale of ivory. The ban has helped elephants.

Today there are about 100,000 elephants left in the world. These animals face many dangers. Some people hunt them illegally. Other people build farms and towns in the places where elephants used to live. As

Game rangers display tusks and weapons taken from men who had been hunting elephants illegally in Zambia.

the animals' natural habitat is destroyed, it gets harder for them to find food.

Elephants digging a hole to find water in a dry riverbed

Elephants play many important roles in their ecosystem. By knocking over trees and eating bushes, they keep grasslands open. This helps zebras, antelope, and other plant eaters.

During dry seasons, elephants dig up riverbeds and find water that many animals can drink. If elephants disappear from Earth, many other animals may vanish too. We must do everything we can to protect elephants.

Will elephants always be part of our world?

To Find Out More

Here are some additional resources to help you learn more about elephants:

 **Books**

Pringle, Laurence. **Elephant Woman: Cynthia Moss Explores the World of Elephants.** Atheneum, 1997.

Smith, Roland and Michael J. Schmidt. **In the Forest with Elephants.** Gulliver Books, 1998.

Stewart, Melissa. **Mammals.** Children's Press, 2001.

Taylor, Barbara. **Elephants.** Lorenz Books, 1999.

Travers, Will. **Elephant.** Raintree/Steck-Vaugn, 1999.

Organizations and Online Sites

African Wildlife Update
4739 Fox Trail Dr. NE
Olympia, Washington
98516
http://www.africanwildlife.org/

This site features up-to-the-minute information about the status of elephants and other threatened and endangered animals that live in Africa.

Elephant Nature Park
http://www.thaifocus.com/elephant/anatomy.htm

This site features all kinds of interesting information about Asian elephants.

Elephant Videos
http://elephant.elehost.com/Multimedia_Page/Videos/duelandmudshort.ram

Watch a variety of videos of elephants in their natural setting in the African country of Botswana.

International Wildlife Coalition
70 East Falmouth Highway
East Falmouth, MA, USA
02536
http://www.iwc.org

The IWC works to save endangered species and preserve animal habitats and the environment.

KidsGoWild
http://wcs.org/sites/kidsgowild

This is the kids' page of the Wildlife Conservation Society. It includes wildlife news, wild animal facts, and information on how kids can get involved in saving wild animals and the environment by joining Conservation Kids.

Important Words

droughts dry periods

ecosystem living things and environmental conditions in the place where a creature lives

lone by oneself

mammal warm-blooded animal that has a backbone and hair and feeds its young mother's milk

matriarch female head of a family group

molars four teeth that an elephant uses to grind its food

musth time when male elephants are tougher than usual and actively looking for mates

predator animal that hunts and kills other animals for food

sparring fighting

Index

Meet the Author

A few years ago, Melissa Stewart visited the African countries of Kenya and Tanzania. While on safari, she had a close encounter with an angry musth elephant that came within 15 feet (4.5 m) of her jeep. Luckily, the huge male quickly lost interest and lumbered away.

Ms. Stewart was entranced by the graceful majesty of the elephants she saw. She spent many hours watching them casually sweep grasses and tree branches into their mouths. She also enjoyed watching one elephant swim in a river, using its long trunk as a snorkel.

Ms. Stewart earned a bachelor's degree in biology from Union College and a master's degree in science and environmental journalism from New York University. She has written more than twenty books for children. Ms. Stewart lives in Marlborough, Massachusetts.

Photographs © 2001: ENP Images/Gerry Ellis: 4, 10 right, 11, 15, 22, 24, 26 left, 26 right, 30, 37; Melissa Stewart: 29; Peter Arnold Inc.: 16 (Dianne Blell), 18, 42 (M. & C. Denis-Huot/BIOS), 13 bottom right (Martin Harvey), 33 (S.J. Krasemann), 14 (Gerard Lacz), 10 left (Fritz Polking); Photo Researchers, NY: 2 (Daryl Balfour/NHPA), 41 (Philip Berry/ABPL), 27 (Jim & Julie Bruton), 31 (Gregory G. Dimijian), 39 (Jack Fields), 9 (M.P. Kahl), cover, 13 left, 20, 25 (Renee Lynn), 6 (E. Hanumantha Rao), 13 top right (Terry Whittaker), 1, 43 (Art Wolfe); Visuals Unlimited: 35 (Francis E. Caldwell), 34 (Gerald & Buff Corsi).